Popular Dog Library

Labrador Retriever

Richard T. Burrows

Published in association with T.F.H. Publications, Inc.,
the world's largest and most respected publisher of pet literature

Chelsea House Publishers
Philadelphia

CONTENTS

Popular Dog Library

Labrador Retriever
Rottweiler
German Shepherd
Golden Retriever
Poodle
Beagle
Dachshund
Cocker Spaniel
Yorkshire Terrier
Pomeranian
Shih Tzu
Chihuahua

Publisher's Note: All of the photographs in this book have been coated with FOTO-GLAZE® finish, a special lamination that imparts a new dimension of colorful gloss to the photographs.

Reinforced Library Binding & Super-Highest Quality Boards

This edition © 1995 TFH Publications, Inc., 1 TFH Plaza, Neptune City, NJ 07753. This special library bound edition is made expressly for Chelsea House Publishers, a division of Main Line Book Company.

Library of Congress Cataloging-in-Publication Data

Burrows, Richard T.
Guide to owning a Labrador retriever / by Richard T. Burrows.
   p.   cm. — (Popular dog library)
Originally published: Neptune City, N.J. : T.F.H. Publications, c1995.
Includes index.
Summary: Discusses choosing a Labrador retriever, the history of the breed, puppy care, grooming, training, and more.
ISBN 0-7910-5470-5 (hc)
1. Labrador retriever Juvenile literature. [1. Labrador retriever. 2. Dogs. 3. Pets.]
I. Title. II. Series.
SF429.L3B87   1999
636.752'7—dc21
                                                                  99-26498
                                                                  CIP

ORIGIN AND HISTORY

According to many authorities, the forebears of the Labrador Retriever were produced in Newfoundland. Authorities generally agree that the breed descended from the St. John's variety of water dog, but attempts to further trace the lineage have failed to produce any coinciding theories.

One school claims Labrador Retrievers were brought to Newfoundland by the fishermen of Devon when they first invaded and settled the land. Another group believes they originated in North America, while still a third asserts they were of Asiatic descent.

The Labrador performed many useful services for the fishermen of Newfoundland—carrying ropes between boats, towing dories, and

These two yellow Labs are Kalalinda Summer Snow and Ravendor Jessie's Last Horrah.

helping gather up fishnets. On several occasions he was even credited with saving crew members from their deaths. The Labrador's stout heart and his faculty for performing numerous and varied tasks earned him a place on many a fishing boat.

LABRADOR IN ENGLAND

The first Labrador was brought to England in the early 1820s, but the breed's reputation had spread to the English shore long before. As the story goes, the Earl of Malmesbury saw a Labrador on a fishing boat and immediately made arrangements with certain traders to have some imported. These first Labradors so impressed the Earl with their genius for retrieving that he devoted his entire kennel to developing and stabilizing the breed. It was not long before many others realized their worth and followed suit; unfortunately, in their enthusiasm they gave little thought to keeping the breed pure. However, the Malmesbury strain retained its purity for many years. Eventually, a combination of the Newfoundland dog tax and the English quarantine laws brought importing practically to a standstill. Interbreeding became necessary as a means of acquiring "fresh blood." In most cases this activity was restricted to the use of the curly-coated and flat-coated retrievers and various strains of water spaniels. Due to the fact that the breed was very old, its characteristics remained predominant throughout.

Finally, in 1903, the Labrador Retriever was recognized by The Kennel Club of England, but at that time no definite standard of conformation was agreed upon. Fortunately for the breed, its followers were primarily interested in the development of working qualities. Unhampered by a standard, they were able to continue their breeding schemes, which included occasional outcrosses, and were responsible for producing the multi-purpose dog that is our present-day Labrador Retriever.

According to records, the Labrador's first appearance in the show ring took place as early as 1860. Strangely enough, this was long before the breed received its official nod from The Kennel Club. There seems to be only one plausible explanation for this phenomenon: the old law of supply and demand. It is said that King George V had a great deal to

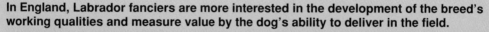

In England, Labrador fanciers are more interested in the development of the breed's working qualities and measure value by the dog's ability to deliver in the field.

do with awakening national interest in the breed.

Then, as now, the majority of the Labrador's followers attributed little importance to success in the show ring. They measured value by the ability to deliver in the field. As a means of discerning their Labrador's respective merits, small groups of enthusiasts started to hold retriever trials in 1880. Over a period of time, the interest and the entries grew considerably. As a result of this increased competition, breeders poured on their efforts to refine and strengthen the Labrador's valuable qualities, each striving to outdo the other. This healthy competition produced the strong foundation that is responsible for the proficient working ability of the breed today.

In the United States the Labrador is the leading field dog as well as one of the 3 most popular breeds.

LABRADOR IN THE UNITED STATES

Americans knew little of the Labrador's true usefulness until after World War I. At that time they gradually began to be imported, but it was not until the mid-1930s that they gained any sort of widespread acclaim. Retriever field trials were largely responsible for the rapid spread of the breed's popularity in the United States. Once the Labrador had the chance to demonstrate his capabilities before the public, his reputation and numbers grew quickly.

The breed has an enormously successful trial record in the United States. For example, during one 20-year period, Labradors placed first in 520 out of the 637 trials open to all breeds of retrievers and Irish Water Spaniels. They have gained the coveted title of National Retriever Champion for 12 out of the first 16 years it was in existence. Little known before the 1930s, the Labrador has already taken an unchallenged lead in the retriever field and today is the country's leading field dog— paws down!

Ch. Aristes' Wish Upon a Star's excellent conformation has earned her not only the title of Champion but many group placements as well.

BREED DESCRIPTION

A breed standard is the criterion by which the appearance (and to a certain extent, the temperament as well) of any given dog is made subject to objective measurement. Basically, the standard for any breed is a definition of the perfect dog, to which all specimens of the breed are compared. Breed standards are subject to change through review by the national breed club for each dog, so it is wise to keep up with developments in a breed by checking the publications of your national kennel club.

AKC STANDARD FOR THE LABRADOR RETRIEVER

General Appearance— The Labrador Retriever is a strongly built, medium-sized, short-coupled dog possessing a sound, athletic, well-balanced conformation that enables it to function as a retrieving gun dog; the substance and soundness to hunt waterfowl or upland game for long hours under difficult conditions; the character and quality to win in the show ring; and the temperament to be a family companion. Physical

The Labrador Retriever is a strongly built, medium-sized hunting dog.

features and mental characteristics should denote a dog bred to perform as an efficient retriever of game with a stable temperament suitable for a variety of pursuits beyond the hunting environment.

The most distinguishing characteristics of the Labrador Retriever are its short, dense, weather resistant coat; an "otter" tail; a clean-cut head with broad back skull and moderate stop; powerful jaws; and its "kind," friendly eyes, expressing character, intelligence and good temperament.

Above all, a Labrador Retriever must be well balanced, enabling it to move in the show ring or work in the field with little or no effort. The typical Labrador possesses style and quality without over refinement, and substance without lumber or cloddiness. The Labrador is bred primarily as a working gun dog; structure and soundness are of great importance.

Size, Proportion and Substance—*Size*—The height at the withers for a dog is 22 $^1/_2$ to 24 $^1/_2$ inches; for a bitch is 21 $^1/_2$ to 23 $^1/_2$ inches. Any variance greater than $^1/_2$ inch above or below these heights is a disqualification. Approximate weight of dogs and bitches in working condition: dogs 65 to 80 pounds; bitches 55 to 70 pounds.

The minimum height ranges set forth in the paragraph above shall not apply to dogs or bitches under twelve months of age.

Proportion—Short-coupled: length from the point of the rump is equal to or slightly longer than the distance from the withers to the ground. Distance from the elbow to the ground should be equal to one half of the height at the withers. The brisket should extend to the elbows, but not perceptibly deeper. The body must be of sufficient length to permit a straight, free and efficient stride; but the dog should never appear low and long or tall and leggy in outline.

Substance—Substance and bone proportionate to the overall dog. Light, "weedy" individuals are definitely incorrect; equally objectionable are cloddy lumbering specimens. Labrador Retrievers shall be shown in working condition, well-muscled and without excess fat.

Head—*Skull*—the skull should be wide; well developed but without exaggeration. The skull and foreface should be on parallel planes and of approximately equal length. There should be a moderate stop—the brow slightly pronounced so that the skull is not absolutely in a straight line with the nose. The brow ridges aid in defining the stop. The head should be clean-cut and free from fleshy cheeks; the bony structure of the skull chiseled beneath the eye with no prominence in the cheek. The skull may show some median line; the occipital bone is not conspicuous in mature dogs. Lips should not be squared off or pendulous, but fall away in a curve toward the throat. A wedge-shaped head, or a head long and narrow in muzzle and back of skull, is incorrect as are massive,

Labradors have kind, friendly eyes expressing their good temperament. Yellow Labradors should have brown eyes and black eye rims.

TOPLINE
Level with a strong back.

TAIL
"Otter" tail. Thick at the base and gradually tapering toward the tip.

HINDLEG
Broad, muscular, and powerful. Strongly boned.

HOCK
Strong and short.

STIFLE
Strong and well-turned.

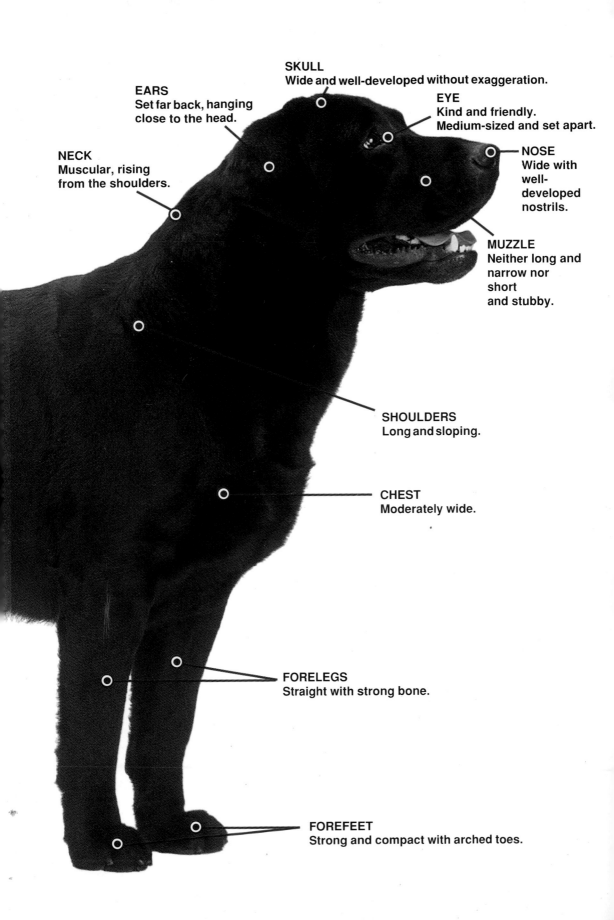

SKULL
Wide and well-developed without exaggeration.

EARS
Set far back, hanging
close to the head.

EYE
Kind and friendly.
Medium-sized and set apart.

NECK
Muscular, rising
from the shoulders.

NOSE
Wide with
well-
developed
nostrils.

MUZZLE
Neither long and
narrow nor
short
and stubby.

SHOULDERS
Long and sloping.

CHEST
Moderately wide.

FORELEGS
Straight with strong bone.

FOREFEET
Strong and compact with arched toes.

cheeky heads. The jaws are powerful and free from snippiness—the muzzle neither long and narrow nor short and stubby. *Nose*—The nose should be wide and the nostrils well developed. The nose should be black on black or yellow dogs, and brown on chocolates. Nose color fading to a lighter shade is not a fault. A thoroughly pink nose or one lacking in any pigment is a disqualification. *Teeth*—the teeth should be strong and regular with a scissors bite; the lower teeth just behind, but touching the inner side of the upper incisors. A level bite is acceptable, but not desirable. Undershot, overshot or misaligned teeth are serious faults. *Ears*—The ears should hang moderately close to the head, set rather far back, and somewhat low on the skull; slightly above eye level. Ears should not be large and heavy, but in proportion with the skull and reach to the inside of the eye when pulled forward. *Eyes*— Kind, friendly eyes imparting good temperament, intelligence and alertness are a hallmark of the breed. They should be of medium size, set well apart, and neither

Chocolate Labs should have a brown nose and brown eyes and eye rims. This is Fudge-a-Muffin's Molly Brown, CD, CGC.

protruding nor deep set. Eye color should be brown in black and yellow Labradors, and brown or hazel in chocolates. Black or yellow eyes give a harsh expression and are undesirable. Small eyes set close together or round prominent eyes are not typical of the breed. Eye rims are black in black and yellow Labradors; and brown in chocolates. Eye rims without pigmentation is a disqualification.

Neck, Topline and Body—*Neck*— The neck should be of proper length to allow the dog to retrieve game easily. It should be muscular and free from throatiness. The neck should rise strongly from the shoulders with a moderate arch. A short, thick neck or a "ewe" neck is incorrect. *Topline*—The back is strong and the topline is level from the withers to the croup when standing or moving. However, the loin should show evidence of flexibility for athletic endeavor. *Body*—The Labrador should be short-coupled, with good spring of ribs tapering to a moderately wide chest. The Labrador should not be narrow chested, giving the appearance of hollowness between the front legs, nor should it have a wide spreading, bulldog-like front. Correct chest conformation will result in tapering between the front legs that allows unrestricted forelimb movement. Chest breadth that is either too wide or too narrow for efficient movement and stamina is incorrect. Slab-sided individuals are not typical of the breed; equally objectionable are rotund or barrel-chested specimens. The underline is almost straight, with little or no tuck-up in mature animals. Loins should be short, wide and strong; extending to well-developed powerful hindquarters. When viewed from the side, the Labrador Retriever shows a well-developed, but not exaggerated forechest. *Tail*—The tail is a distinguishing feature of the breed. It should be very thick at the base, gradually tapering toward the tip, of medium length, and extending no longer than to the hock. The tail should be free from feathering and clothed thickly all around with the Labrador's short, dense coat, thus having that particular rounded appearance that has been described as the "otter" tail. The tail should follow the topline in repose or when in motion. It may be carried gaily, but should not curl over the back. Extremely short tails or long thin tails are serious faults. The tail completes

Dogs are measured from the shoulders to the ground. The height of the Labrador Retriever male should be 22 $\frac{1}{2}$ to 24 $\frac{1}{2}$ inches; bitches should be 21 $\frac{1}{2}$ to 23 $\frac{1}{2}$ inches. Drawing by John Quinn.

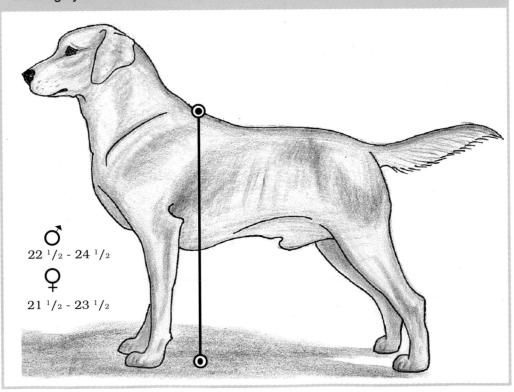

♂
22 $^{1}/_{2}$ - 24 $^{1}/_{2}$

♀
21 $^{1}/_{2}$ - 23 $^{1}/_{2}$

the balance of the Labrador by giving it a flowing line from the top of the head to the tip of the tail. Docking or otherwise altering the length or natural carriage of the tail is a disqualification.

Forequarters—Forequarters should be muscular, well coordinated and balanced with the hindquarters. *Shoulders*—The shoulders are well laid-back, long and sloping, forming an angle with the upper arm of approximately 90 degrees that permits the dog to move his forelegs in an easy manner with strong forward reach. Ideally, the length of the shoulder blade should equal the length of the upper arm. Straight shoulder blades, short upper arms or heavily muscled or loaded shoulders, all restricting free movement, are incorrect. *Front legs*—When viewed from the front, the legs should be straight with good strong bone. Too much bone is as undesirable as too little bone, and short-legged, heavy-boned individuals are not typical of the breed. Viewed from the side, the elbows should be directly under the withers, and the front legs should be perpendicular to the ground and well under the body. The elbows should be close to the ribs without looseness. Tied-in elbows or being "out at the elbows" interfere with free movement and are serious faults. Pasterns should be strong and short and should slope slightly from the perpendicular line of the leg. Feet are strong and compact, with well-arched toes and well-developed pads. Dew claws may be removed. Splayed feet, hare feet, knuckling over, or feet turning in or out are serious faults.

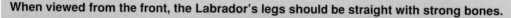

When viewed from the front, the Labrador's legs should be straight with strong bones.

The otter tail is a requirement for the Labrador Retriever. It is a strong tail, thick at the base and tapering toward the tip, densely coated with thick, short fur; flat on the underside, rounded in section and specifically constructed to act as a rudder whilst swimming. Drawing by John Quinn

Hindquarters—The Labrador's hindquarters are broad, muscular and well-developed from the hip to the hock with well-turned stifles and strong short hocks. Viewed from the rear, the hind legs are straight and parallel. Viewed from the side, the angulation of the rear legs is in balance with the front. The hind legs are strongly boned, muscled with moderate angulation at the stifle, and powerful, clearly defined thighs. The stifle is strong and there is no slippage of the patella while in motion or when standing. The hock joints are strong, well let down and do not slip or hyper-extend while in motion or when standing. Angulation of both stifle and hock joint is such as to achieve the optimal balance of drive and traction. When standing the rear toes are only slightly behind the point of the rump. Over-

angulation produces a sloping topline not typical of the breed. Feet are strong and compact, with well-arched toes and well-developed pads. Cow-hocks, spread hocks, sickle hocks and over-angulation are serious structural defects and are to be faulted.

Coat—The coat is a distinctive feature of the Labrador Retriever. It should be short, straight and very dense, giving a fairly hard feeling to the hand. The Labrador should have a soft, weather-resistant undercoat that provides protection from water, cold and all types of ground cover. A slight

Cow hocks are a serious structural fault in the Labrador Retriever and must be faulted. Drawing by John Quinn.

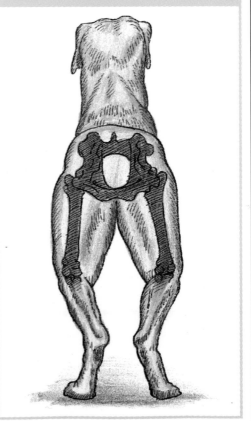

wave down the back is permissible. Woolly coats are not typical of the breed, and should be severely penalized.

Color—The Labrador Retriever coat colors are black, yellow and chocolate. Any other color or a combination of colors is a disqualification. A small white spot on the chest is permissible, but not desirable. White hairs from aging or scarring are not to be misinterpreted as brindling. *Black*—Blacks are all black. A black with brindle markings or a black with tan markings is a disqualification. *Yellow*—Yellows may range in color from fox-red to light cream, with variations in shading on the ears, back and underparts of the dog. *Chocolate*—Chocolates can vary in shade from light to dark chocolate. Chocolate with brindle or tan markings is a disqualification.

Movement—Movement of the Labrador Retriever should be free and effortless. When watching a dog move toward oneself, there should be no sign of elbows out. Rather, the elbows should be held neatly to the body with the legs not too close together. Moving straight forward without pacing or weaving, the legs should form straight lines, with all parts moving in the same plane. Upon viewing the dog from the rear, one should have the impression that the hind legs move as nearly as possible in a parallel line with the front legs. The hocks should do their full share of the work,

The Labrador Retriever comes in three colors: black, yellow, and chocolate (brown).

flexing well, giving the appearance of power and strength. When viewed from the side, the shoulders should move freely and effortlessly, and the foreleg should reach forward close to the ground with extension. A short, choppy movement or high knee action indicates a straight shoulder; paddling indicates long, weak pasterns; and a short, stilted rear gait indicates a straight rear assembly: all are serious faults. Movement faults interfering with performance, including weaving; side-winding; crossing over; high knee action; paddling; and short, choppy movement, should be severely penalized.

Temperament—True Labrador Retriever temperament is as much a hallmark of the breed as the "otter" tail. The ideal disposition is one of a kindly, outgoing, tractable nature; eager to please and non-aggressive towards man or animal. The Labrador has much that appeals to people: his gentle ways, intelligence and adaptability make him an ideal dog. Aggressiveness towards humans or other animals, or any evidence of shyness in an adult, should be severely penalized.

DISQUALIFICATIONS

1. Any deviation from the height prescribed in the Standard.

2. A thoroughly pink nose or one lacking in any pigment.

3. Eye rims without pigment.

4. Docking or otherwise altering the length or natural carriage of the tail.

5. Any other color or a combination of colors other than black, yellow or chocolate as described in the Standard.

The Labrador has proven his worth in all fields of work. Here, Indy Corson skis in as Labrador Retriever Rex starts to dig for an avalanche victim.

TEMPERAMENT AND PERSONALITY

The reason for the Labrador's continued popularity is that over the years he has consistently proven his worth in all fields and truly earned the title "all around" dog.

One of the most predominant characteristics of the Labrador is a strong desire to please. This quality has done much to enhance the breed's popularity. Coupled with a high degree of natural intelligence, it equips the Labrador to fulfill the roles of hunter, retriever, companion, pet and watchdog. This desire to please makes the Labrador a willing and eager pupil, a dog that enjoys learning and is a pleasure to teach.

By far the most exciting of the Labrador's qualities is his

Another endearing characteristic of the breed is its untiring devotion to people. The Labrador thrives on human company and companionship; he has the rare ability of being able to be everybody's friend and still maintain an undying allegiance to his master.

The Labrador has the uncanny

A Labrador retrieves a pigeon through decoys. The Labrador's inherent working ability is one of his most exciting qualities.

inherent working ability. This all-important factor has been maintained and strengthened over the years by careful and selective breeding. So strong is the Labrador's natural inclination for retrieving that it is manifested when a puppy is still under three months of age.

and most admirable quality of being able to adapt himself to all sorts of situations and surroundings. His devotion and patience make him a trusted playmate for children. He joins in their games with enthusiasm and thoroughly enjoys what you and I would consider mauling. At the

One of the roles of the Labrador Retriever as a detector dog is searching suitcases for drugs as shown at this outdoor demonstration.

same time, he is perfectly able to take care of himself by simply evacuating the area if things get too rough. Somehow, in each instance, the Labrador seems to grasp almost instinctively what is desired and to willingly apply himself in that direction.

Few other breeds can match the Labrador for perseverance and courage. His reputation was founded on his ability to withstand the hardships of a day's shoot. Whether it is retrieving ducks in icy water on a cold winter day or hunting pheasants in honeysuckle groves, hedgerows, briar patches, and other likely spots, the Labrador performs his task like a trooper. How much wounded game would have been lost if it were not for the Labrador's excellent scenting powers and perseverance! Any duck hunter knows the trouble strong, wounded game can cause, but the Labrador does not give up. Certain members of the breed have been known to carry on hot pursuit for over an hour.

The Labrador's coat sheds water quickly and also protects him from burrs and briars.

THE LABRADOR'S APPEARANCE

The Labrador's body and coat fit him so well for both indoor and outdoor life that they seem to have been designed by a master craftsman. He has a rugged appearance, standing about 2 feet high, being fairly long and very solid in body, with a good head, thick neck, deep chest, and well-developed legs. Even his tail contributes to his work. While he is swimming, it acts as a rudder, and when he is working the upland, it waves like a flag, signaling when he is marking game. His "polished" coat sheds water quickly and protects him from burrs and briars, enabling him to get through the thickest of cover.

All told, the Labrador's many admirable qualities render him truly a dog of distinction. So long as there remains a person who values loyalty and courage, the Labrador will have a friend.

TRIBUTES TO THE BREED

Anyone who has ever shot over a Labrador knows the thrill that comes from watching this dog at work. So great is the Labrador's love of his profession that his entire personality changes at just the sight of a gun being taken out of the closet. His excitement is intense, and from that first moment until departure time he never leaves his shooting partner's side by more than a few feet.

The dog's enthusiasm is so strong that it affects all those who come into contact with him, greatly increasing their enjoyment of the sport. But with this added impetus comes a conscience, for it does not take the Labrador long to wise up to the fact that you, too, have your bad days, and his subsequent disappointment will affect you far more than your own disgust.

We have a wonderful old bitch who was brought into the family as a pup. Her shooting experiences had always been with my father until, on this one day,

A line up of Labrador Retrievers practice honoring, which means remaining steady while another dog is sent to retrieve.

A Labrador Retriever search and rescue dog is given a scent to follow.

As evidence of the breed's intelligence, supersensitive nose, and devotion to masters is the following story of a Labrador who was left alone in a strange place. The incident took place on a night's stop during the return from a shooting trip. The dog was taken by car to a strange kennel, approximately three miles from the strange house. He had a good view of the road and watched his master's car until it disappeared. During the night he succeeded in climbing out of his pen and making his way to the house, but he had no way of getting inside. So he tried to do the next best thing, get into the car. Here again his efforts were thwarted, as it was locked. He finally settled for sleeping under the car, satisfied that was the nearest to his master he could get.

Being extremely perceptive by nature, the Labrador is able to sense human moods almost instantaneously. In black moments, when everything seems to be going wrong, he has a very amusing way of showing his affection that cannot help but bring a smile.

All Labrador fans should be especially proud of the way in which the breed has distinguished itself in extracurricular activities. In World War II the Labrador gained the reputation of being able to detect land mines in less time and with more consistency than any other breed. They have performed so successfully as guide dogs for the blind that today they are currently the most preferred breed.

she was loaned to another couple in the same ducking group. Their blind was on the end of a point, about half a mile distant from my father's position. Everything was in readiness well before dawn, and with the first signs of light the ducks began to move. For some reason that morning the point blind saw very little action, and to make it worse the people in it promptly muffed the few chances they had. About an hour of this was all the old bitch could stand. She waited for her chance and then slipped away. Ten minutes later a black head was in the water, approaching my unaware father's blind.

YOUR NEW LABRADOR PUPPY

SELECTION

When you do pick out a Labrador Retriever puppy as a pet, don't be hasty; the longer you study puppies, the better you will eagerly to make and to cultivate your acquaintance. Don't fall for any shy little darling that wants to retreat to his bed or his box, or plays coy behind other puppies or

Before you choose your Labrador, study the puppies long and hard.

understand them. Make it your transcendent concern to select only one that radiates good health and spirit and is lively on his feet, whose eyes are bright, whose coat shines, and who comes forward people, or hides his head under your arm or jacket appealing to your protective instinct. *Pick the Labrador Retriever puppy who forthrightly picks you! The feeling of attraction should be mutual!*

DOCUMENTS

Now, a little paper work is in order. When you purchase a purebred Labrador Retriever puppy, you should receive a transfer of ownership, registration material, and other "papers" (a list of the immunization shots, if any, the puppy may have been given; a note on whether or not the puppy has been wormed; a diet and feeding schedule to which the puppy is accustomed) and you are welcomed as a fellow owner to a long, pleasant association with a most lovable pet, and more (news)paper work.

GENERAL PREPARATION

You have chosen to own a particular Labrador Retriever puppy. You have chosen it very carefully over all other breeds and all other puppies. So before you ever get that Labrador Retriever puppy home, you will have prepared for its arrival by reading everything you can get your hands on having to do with the management of Labrador Retrievers and puppies. True, you will run into many conflicting opinions, but at least you will not be starting "blind." Read, study, digest. Talk over your plans with your veterinarian, other "Labrador Retriever people," and the seller of your Labrador Retriever puppy.

When you get your Labrador Retriever puppy, you will find that your reading and study are far from finished. You've just scratched the surface in your plan to provide the greatest possible comfort and health for your Labrador Retriever; and, by the same token, you do want to assure yourself of the greatest possible enjoyment of this wonderful creature. You must be ready for this puppy mentally as well as in the physical requirements.

When picking your new Labrador puppy, it is a good idea, whenever possible, to see how he interacts with his littermates. This pair seems to be on the adventurous side.

TRANSPORTATION

If you take the puppy home by car, protect him from drafts, particularly in cold weather. Wrapped in a towel and carried in the arms or lap of a passenger, the Labrador Retriever puppy will usually make the trip without mishap. If the pup starts to drool and to squirm, stop the car for a few minutes. Have newspapers handy in case of car-sickness. A covered carton lined with newspapers provides protection for puppy and car, if you are driving alone. Avoid excitement and unnecessary handling of the puppy on arrival. A Labrador Retriever puppy is a very small "package" to be making a complete change of surroundings and company, and he needs frequent rest and refreshment to renew his vitality.

THE FIRST DAY AND NIGHT

When your Labrador Retriever puppy arrives in your home, put him down on the floor and don't pick him up again, except when it is absolutely necessary. He is a dog, a real dog, and must not be lugged around like a rag doll. Handle him as little as possible, and permit no one to pick him up and baby him. To repeat, *put your Labrador Retriever puppy on the floor or the ground and let him stay there except when it may be necessary to do otherwise.*

Quite possibly your Labrador Retriever puppy will be afraid for a while in his new surroundings, without his mother and littermates. Comfort him and reassure him, but don't console him. Don't give him the "oh-you-poor-itsy-bitsy-puppy" treatment. Be calm, friendly, and reassuring. Encourage him to walk around and sniff over his new home. If it's dark, put on the lights. Let him roam for a few minutes while you and everyone else concerned sit quietly or go about your routine business. Let the puppy come back to you.

Playmates may cause an immediate problem if the new Labrador Retriever puppy is to be greeted by children or other pets. If not, you can skip this subject. The natural affinity between puppies and children calls for some supervision until a live-and-let-live relationship is established. This applies particularly to a Christmas puppy, when there is more excitement than usual and more chance for a puppy to swallow something upsetting. It is

When you bring your Lab puppy home, make him feel as comfortable and relaxed as possible. He will need time to adjust to his new surroundings.

You should have a soft, warm bed available for your new Lab pup.

a better plan to welcome the puppy several days before or after the holiday week. Like a baby, your Labrador Retriever puppy needs much rest and should not be over-handled. Once a child realizes that a puppy has "feelings" similar to his own, and can readily be hurt or injured, the opportunities for play and responsibilities provide exercise and training for both.

For his first night with you, he should be put where he is to sleep every night—say in the kitchen, since its floor can usually be

Nine-week-old Labrador Retriever puppies.

easily cleaned. Let him explore the kitchen to his heart's content; close doors to confine him there. Prepare his food and feed him lightly the first night. Give him a pan with some water in it—not a lot, since most puppies will try to drink the whole pan dry. Give him an old coat or shirt to lie on. Since a coat or shirt will be strong in human scent, he will pick it out to lie on, thus furthering his feeling of security in the room where he has just been fed.

HOUSEBREAKING HELPS

Now, sooner or later—mostly sooner—your new Labrador Retriever puppy is going to "puddle" on the floor. First take a newspaper and lay it on the puddle until the urine is soaked up onto the paper. *Save this paper.* Now take a cloth with soap and water, wipe up the floor and dry it well. Then take the wet paper and place it on a fairly large square of newspapers in a convenient corner. When cleaning up, always keep a piece of wet paper on top of the others. Every time he wants to "squat," he will seek out this spot and use the papers. (This routine is rarely necessary for more than three days.) Now leave your Labrador Retriever puppy for the night. Quite probably he will cry and howl a bit; some are more stubborn than others on this matter. But let him stay alone for the night. This may seem harsh treatment, but it is the best procedure in the long run. Just let him cry; he will weary of it sooner or later.

FEEDING

Now let's talk about feeding your Labrador Retriever, a subject so simple that it's amazing there is so much nonsense and misunderstanding about it. Is it expensive to feed a Labrador do not have a high degree of selectivity in their food, and unless you spoil them with great variety (and possibly turn them into poor, "picky" eaters) they will eat almost anything that they

Feeding your Labrador human food directly off of your plate is not a good idea. Rich human foods may upset his stomach, and this practice encourages begging.

Retriever? No, it is not! You can feed your Labrador Retriever economically and keep him in perfect shape the year round, or you can feed him expensively. He'll thrive either way, and let's see why this is true.

First of all, remember a Labrador Retriever is a dog. Dogs become accustomed to. Many dogs flatly refuse to eat nice, fresh beef. They pick around it and eat everything else. But meat—bah! Why? They aren't accustomed to it! They'd eat rabbit fast enough, but they refuse beef because they aren't used to it.

Your Labrador should be provided with clean, fresh water at all times.

VARIETY NOT NECESSARY

A good general rule of thumb is forget all human preferences and don't give a thought to variety. Choose the right diet for your Labrador Retriever and feed it to him day after day, year after year, winter and summer. But what is the right diet?

Hundreds of thousands of dollars have been spent in canine nutrition research. The results are pretty conclusive, so you needn't go into a lot of experimenting with trials of this and that every other week. Research has proven just what your dog needs to eat and to keep healthy.

DOG FOOD

There are almost as many right diets as there are dog experts, but the basic diet most often recommended is one that consists of a dry food, either meal or kibble form. There are several of excellent quality, manufactured by reliable companies, research tested, and nationally advertised. They are inexpensive, highly satisfactory, and easily available in stores everywhere in containers of five to 50 pounds. Larger amounts cost less per pound, usually.

If you have a choice of brands, it is usually safer to choose the better known one; but even so, carefully read the analysis on the package. Do not choose any food in which the protein level is less than 25 percent, and be sure that this protein comes from both animal and vegetable sources. The good dog foods have meat meal, fish meal, liver, and such, plus protein from alfalfa and soybeans, as well as some dried-milk product. Note the vitamin content carefully. See that they are all there in good proportions; and be especially certain that the food contains properly high levels of vitamins A and D, two of the most perishable and important ones. Note the B-complex level, but don't worry about carbohydrate and mineral levels. These substances are plentiful and cheap and not likely to be lacking in a good brand.

The advice given for how to choose a dry food also applies to moist or canned types of dog foods, if you decide to feed one of these.

Having chosen a really good food, feed it to your Labrador Retriever as the manufacturer directs. And once you've started, stick to it. Never change if you can possibly help it. A switch from one meal or kibble-type food can usually be made without too much upset; however, a change will almost invariably give you (and your Labrador Retriever) some trouble.

Puppies need to follow a strict schedule for food and water, especially during housebreaking.

WHEN SUPPLEMENTS ARE NEEDED

Now what about supplements of various kinds, mineral and vitamin, or the various oils? They are all okay to add to your Labrador Retriever's food. However, if you are feeding your Labrador Retriever a correct diet, and this is easy to do, no supplements are necessary unless your Labrador Retriever has been improperly fed, has been sick, or is having puppies. Vitamins and minerals are naturally present in all the foods; and to ensure against any loss through processing, they are added in concentrated form to the dog food you use. Except on the advice of your veterinarian, added amounts of vitamins can prove harmful to your Labrador Retriever! The same risk goes with minerals.

FEEDING SCHEDULE

When and how much food to give your Labrador Retriever? As to when (except in the instance of puppies), suit yourself. You may feed two meals per day or the same amount in one single feeding, either morning or night. As to how to prepare the food and how much to give, it is generally best to follow the directions on the food package. Your own Labrador Retriever may want a little more or a little less.

Fresh, cool water should teeth and jaws are developing—for cutting the puppy teeth, to induce growth of the permanent teeth under the puppy teeth, to assist in getting rid of the puppy teeth at the proper time, to help the permanent teeth through the gums, to ensure normal jaw development, and to settle the permanent teeth solidly in the jaws.

The adult Labrador Retriever's desire to chew stems from the instinct for tooth cleaning, gum massage, and jaw exercise—plus

Puppies need something to chew on during the teething period. Encourage constructive chewing by providing your Labrador pup with a Gumabone®.

always be available to your Labrador Retriever. This is important to good health throughout his lifetime.

ALL LABRADOR RETRIEVERS NEED TO CHEW

Puppies and young Labrador Retrievers need something with resistance to chew on while their the need for an outlet for periodic doggie tensions.

This is why dogs, especially puppies and young dogs, will often destroy property worth hundreds of dollars when their chewing instinct is not diverted from their owner's possessions. And this is why you should provide your Labrador Retriever

This Labrador proudly shows off his Nylafloss®. Even though your dog may not believe you, Nylafloss® is not a toy but a most effective agent in controlling plaque.

Pet shops sell real bones which have been colored, cooked, dyed or served natural. Some of the bones are huge, but they usually are easily destroyed by Labradors and become very dangerous.

with something to chew—something that has the necessary functional qualities, is desirable from the Labrador Retriever's viewpoint, and is safe for him.

It is very important that your Labrador Retriever not be permitted to chew on anything he can break or on any indigestible thing from which he can bite sizable chunks. Sharp pieces, such as from a bone which can be broken by a dog, may pierce the intestinal wall and kill. Indigestible things that can be bitten off in chunks, such as from shoes or rubber or plastic toys, may cause an intestinal stoppage (if not regurgitated) and bring painful death, unless surgery is promptly performed.

A chicken-flavored Gumabone has tiny particles of chicken powder embedded in it to keep the Labrador interested.

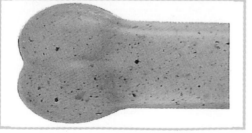

Strong natural bones, such as 4- to 8-inch lengths of round shin bone from mature beef—either the kind you can get from a butcher or one of the variety available commercially in pet stores—may serve your Labrador Retriever's teething needs if his mouth is large enough to handle them effectively. You may be tempted to give your Labrador Retriever puppy a smaller bone and he may not be able to break it when you do, but puppies grow rapidly and the power of their jaws constantly increases until maturity. This means that a growing Labrador Retriever may break one of the

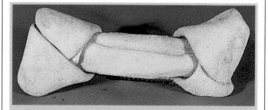

Rawhide is probably the best-selling dog chew. It can be dangerous and cause a dog to choke on it as it swells when wet. A molded, melted rawhide mixed with casein is available (though always scarce). This is the only suitable rawhide for Labradors.

smaller bones at any time, swallow the pieces, and die painfully before you realize what is wrong.

All hard natural bones are very abrasive. If your Labrador Retriever is an avid chewer, natural bones may wear away his teeth prematurely; hence, they then should be taken away from your dog when the teething purposes have been served. The badly worn, and usually painful, teeth of many mature dogs can be traced to excessive chewing on natural bones.

Most pet shops have complete walls dedicated to safe pacifiers.

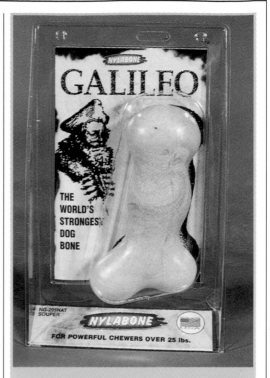

The Galileo is an extremely tough nylon pacifier. Its design is based upon original sketches by Galileo. A book explaining the history and workings of the design come inside each package. This might very well be the best design for a Labrador Retriever.

Contrary to popular belief, knuckle bones that can be chewed up and swallowed by your Labrador Retriever provide little, if any, usable calcium or other nutriment. They do, however, disturb the digestion of most dogs and cause them to vomit the nourishing food they need.

Dried rawhide products of various types, shapes, sizes, and prices are available on the market and have become quite popular. However, they don't serve the primary chewing functions very

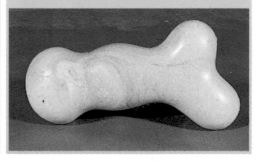

Raised dental tips on each dog bone works wonders with controlling plaque in a Labrador Retrievers.

Only get the largest plaque attacker for your Labrador.

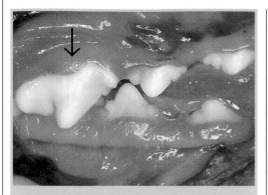

In a scientific study, this shows a dog's tooth (arrow) while being maintained by Gumabone® chewing.

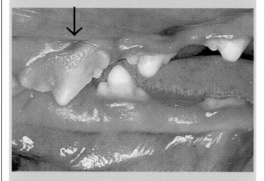

The Gumabone® was taken away and in 30 days the tooth was almost completely covered with plaque and tartar.

well; they are a bit messy when wet from mouthing, and most Labrador Retrievers chew them up rather rapidly—but they have been considered safe for dogs until recently. Now, more and more incidents of death, and near death, by strangulation have been reported to be the results of partially swallowed chunks of rawhide swelling in the throat. More recently, some veterinarians have been attributing cases of acute constipation to large pieces of incompletely digested rawhide in the intestine.

A new product, molded rawhide, is very safe. During the process, the rawhide is melted and then injection molded into the familiar dog shape. It is very hard and is eagerly accepted by Labrador Retrievers. The melting process also sterilizes the rawhide. Don't confuse this with pressed rawhide, which is nothing more than small strips of rawhide squeezed together.

The nylon bones, especially those with natural meat and bone fractions added, are probably the most complete, safe, and economical answer to the chewing need. Dogs cannot break them or bite off sizable chunks; hence, they are completely safe—and

The nylon tug toy is actually a dental floss. You grab one end and let your Labrador Retriever tug on the other as it slowly slips through his teeth since nylon is self-lubricating (slippery). Do NOT use cotton rope tug toys as cotton is organic and rots. It is also weak and easily loses strands which are indigestible should the dog swallow them.

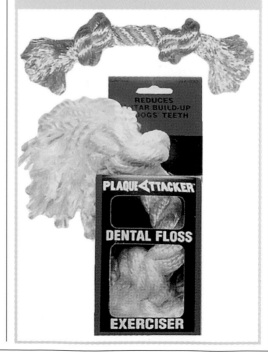

being longer lasting than other things offered for the purpose, they are economical.

Hard chewing raises little bristle-like projections on the surface of the nylon bones—to provide effective interim tooth cleaning and vigorous gum massage, much in the same way your toothbrush does it for you. The little projections are raked off and swallowed in the form of thin shavings, but the chemistry of the nylon is such that they break down in the stomach fluids and pass through without effect.

The toughness of the nylon provides the strong chewing resistance needed for important jaw exercise and effectively aids teething functions, but there is no tooth wear because nylon is non-abrasive. Being inert, nylon does not support the growth of microorganisms; and it can be washed in soap and water or it can be sterilized by boiling or in an autoclave.

Nylabone® is highly recommended by veterinarians as a safe, healthy nylon bone that can't splinter or chip. Nylabone® is frizzled by the dog's chewing action, creating a toothbrush-like surface that cleanses the teeth and massages the gums. Nylabone®, the only chew products made of flavor-impregnated solid nylon, are available in your local pet shop. Nylabone® is superior to the cheaper bones because it is made of virgin nylon, which is the strongest

Labrador Retriever relaxing with his Gumabone®. These chew toys come in a variety of colors and shapes, and dogs love to chew them.

and longest-lasting type of nylon available. The cheaper bones are made from recycled or re-ground nylon scraps, and have a tendency to break apart and split easily.

Nothing, however, substitutes for periodic professional attention for your Labrador Retriever's teeth and gums, not any more than your toothbrush can do that for you. Have your Labrador Retriever's teeth cleaned at least once a year by your veterinarian (twice a year is better) and he will be happier, healthier, and far more pleasant to live with.

Labrador Retrievers have a great amount of strength and stamina. These two yellow Labs are having a friendly wrestling match.

EXERCISE AND ENVIRONMENT

Although the Labrador has a wonderful ability to adjust himself to almost any sort of condition or surroundings, there are a few essentials necessary to his development and well being that we as owners and dog lovers must grant him.

EXERCISE

To fit him for his role of hunter and retriever, the Labrador has been endowed with a great amount of strength and stamina. Whether you plan to hunt your dog or simply utilize his capacity as a friend and companion, you must see to it that he gets ample opportunity for exercise.

If you live in a city or large town and your only means of exercising are leash and collar promenades, the Labrador is not the dog for you. He was not meant for that sort of existence any more than the proverbial fish deprived of water. To maintain health and happiness and properly develop his body, the Labrador must have at least 15 minutes of unrestricted exercise twice a day.

GENERAL CARE

The Labrador provides a bottomless source of companionship, pleasure, and love. In return, the least we can do is to protect his rights by

To maintain the health and happiness of your Labrador, provide at least 15 minutes of unrestricted exercise twice a day.

Labrador Retrievers love the great outdoors. Here a trio of Labs plays tug-of-war with a stick. Remember, chewing on branches can be hazardous to your dog.

ensuring his physical and mental comfort. The basis of mental comfort is simple: it is merely a mutual understanding and respect. The main dangers to it are:

1. Loss of temper, resulting in harsh treatment.

2. Punishing the dog for something he does not understand.

3. Attempting to teach him too many things too soon, and for periods too long in time.

4. Allowing children to abuse him.

Proper sleeping quarters have a great deal to do with maintaining a dog's health. Of primary importance is that the bed be free from drafts and dampness.

In the summer, special care should be taken to see that there is a shady spot in the yard at all times of the day. A platform about a foot and a half high will provide the necessary shade and also give him a place to lie when the ground is cold and wet.

If you must take your Labrador in the car with you, make sure to leave windows at least partially open so there is cross ventilation, and park in a spot that is shady and will remain shady for the duration of your absence. Leaving a dog in a car during the summer is a *very* bad idea. It takes but ten minutes for a dog to be overcome by heatstroke so leaving a dog in a car is usually not worth the risk.

TRAINING

You owe proper training to your Labrador Retriever. The right and privilege of being trained is his birthright; and whether your Labrador Retriever is going to be a handsome, well-mannered housedog and companion, a show dog, or whatever possible use he may be put to, the basic training is always the same—all must start and polite wherever he goes; he must be polite to strangers on the street and in stores. He must be mannerly in the presence of other dogs. He must not bark at children on roller skates, motorcycles, or other domestic animals. And he must be restrained from chasing cats. It is not a dog's inalienable right to

With basic obedience training, you can be sure that your Labrador will be mannerly and polite wherever he goes.

with basic obedience, or what might be called "manner training."

Your Labrador Retriever must come instantly when called and obey the "Sit" or "Down" command just as fast; he must walk quietly at "Heel," whether on or off lead. He must be mannerly chase cats, and he must be reprimanded for it.

PROFESSIONAL TRAINING

How do you go about this training? Well, it's a very simple procedure, pretty well standardized by now. First, if you can afford the extra expense, you may send your Labrador Retriever to a professional trainer, where in 30 to 60 days he will learn how to be a "good dog." If you enlist the services of a good professional trainer, follow his advice of when to come to see the dog. No, he won't forget you, but too-frequent visits at the wrong time may slow down his training progress. And using a "pro" trainer means that you will have to go for some training, too, after the trainer feels your Labrador Retriever is ready to go home. You will have to learn how your Labrador Retriever works,

Retractable leashes are the preferred type for well-trained Labrador Retrievers. The Trakt enables you to adjust the length of the leash. Photo courtesy of Hagen.

just what to expect of him and how to use what the dog has learned after he is home.

OBEDIENCE TRAINING CLASS

Another way to train your Labrador Retriever (many experienced Labrador Retriever people think this is the best) is to join an obedience training class right in your own community. There is such a group in nearly every community nowadays. Here you will be working with a group of people who are also just starting out. You will actually be training your own dog, since all work is done under the direction of a head trainer who will make suggestions to you and also tell you when and how to correct your Labrador Retriever's errors. Then, too, working with such a group, your Labrador Retriever will learn to get along with other dogs. And, what is more important, he will learn to do exactly what he is told to do, no matter how much confusion there is around him or how great the temptation is to go his own way.

Write to your national kennel club for the location of a training club or class in your locality. Sign up. Go to it regularly— every session! Go early and leave late! Both you and your Labrador Retriever will benefit tremendously.

TRAIN HIM BY THE BOOK

The third way of training your Labrador Retriever is by the book. Yes, you can do it this way and do a good job of it too. But in using the book method, select a book, buy it, study it carefully; then study it some more, until the procedures are almost second nature to you. Then start your training. But stay with the book and its advice and exercises. Don't start in and then make up a few rules of your own. If you don't follow the book, you'll get into jams you can't get out of by yourself. If after a few hours of short training sessions your Labrador Retriever is still not working as he should, get back to the book for a study session, because it's your fault, not the dog's! The

SUCCESSFUL DOG TRAINING is one of the better dog training books by Hollywood dog trainer Michael Kamer, who trains dogs for movie stars.

procedures of dog training have been so well systemized that it must be your fault, since literally thousands of fine Labrador Retrievers have been trained by the book.

After your Labrador Retriever is "letter perfect" under all conditions, then, if you wish, go on to advanced training and trick work.

Your Labrador Retriever will love his obedience training, and you'll burst with pride at the finished product! Your Labrador Retriever will enjoy life even more, and you'll enjoy your Labrador Retriever more. And remember—you *owe good training to your Labrador Retriever.*

Marsh Dak's Shooting Star, CD, a black Labrador Retriever in an advanced obedience class.

A boat bumper or fender with a rope tied to the end of it makes a perfect training dummy for retrieving lessons.

TRAINING FOR RETRIEVING

This phase of training should not be started until the dog is over six months old and should not include more than two or three retrieves a day for the first few months. There are two things that must be accomplished early in a Labrador's career. First, his work must become the most exciting thing in his life, and secondly, his hunting instinct must be developed. There is only one way in which these things can be satisfactorily established, and that is by the strict rationing of daily work allotments.

The Lab is one of the finest hunting dogs you could ever own, for he has natural retrieving instincts that are just waiting to be developed.

The act of retrieving must be associated with a command. Whether you choose "Get back!," "Get out!" or the dog's name as your signal, it must be accompanied by a hand motion in the direction of the fall and be used before each retrieve.

Boat fenders or bumpers are the most satisfactory things to use for the early lessons. They are the perfect shape, come in varying weights, and do for land and water retrieves. About 6 inches of clothesline tied on to the end of the fender will make it easier to manipulate and greatly increase the distance it can be thrown.

The first step is to introduce the puppy to the training dummy. This should be made as exciting as possible. A playful voice and teasing actions build up the suspense. When his enthusiasm reaches the boiling point, hurl the dummy out about 20 feet. The instant he reaches it, start blowing the "Come!" whistle, at the same time clapping your hands and running away. (These antics are necessary to ensure a speedy return.) Once he has has caught up to you, reach down and take the dummy gently. Praise him thoroughly and then repeat the action, this time throwing it a bit farther.

For the first few days the lessons should take place on bare ground or a lawn. As soon as the puppy comprehends the retrieving principle, you can move to a spot that has just enough cover to conceal the dummy. From now on, the puppy should be held and not given the command to retrieve until the dummy hits the ground. Gradually increase the distance of the retrieves when his past performance shows that he has mastered the present length. The same principle applies to the use of higher and thicker types of cover.

If in the course of training he should have trouble finding the dummy and heads back toward you, ignore him. Nine times out of ten, as soon as he sees that help is not forthcoming, he will return to the job. This is important because it is the only way to develop perseverance. Once he gets accustomed to receiving help, he will ask for it whenever the going gets tough. Needless to say, this is an undesirable trait and most difficult to overcome once it has been set.

Training your Labrador for retrieving should not commence until the dog is over six months of age. Although he is still too young for this type of training, this little pup is showing his instincts at an early age.

INTRODUCTION TO WATER

Before the puppy is asked to do any kind of work in the water, he should have a pleasant and gradual introduction.

About the most successful way to accomplish this is to enlist the aid of a good water dog; throw a dummy and let your dog follow the other dog at will. After you have repeated this several times to everyone's satisfaction, try your dog alone on a short retrieve, releasing him before the dummy has landed. If he fails to enter the water promptly, release the veteran again to set the example.

A great many lessons can be taught using this method. You will find that a dog, like a child, learns some things more quickly through imitation. Also, the presence of competition will increase your dog's enthusiasm and should do away with any doubts he might have concerning the new adventure.

If a reliable water dog is not available, one of several other methods can be employed. One way is to place yourself across a small stretch of water from the dog and then call him to you. Another way is to set the example yourself by wading into the water and calling your dog. You may also get into a rowboat and coax the dog to swim out to you.

RETRIEVING IN WATER

The first few times, toss the dummy close to the shore and let the puppy go after it while it is still in the air. The second he has it, start blowing your whistle furiously and moving backwards. This should avoid the possibility of his dropping it on the shore. Once he has the idea, you can follow the same length-increasing schedule as used for land work.

LONGER RETRIEVES

For this purpose it is necessary to enlist the aid of a helper. Be sure the helper understands the importance of throwing high in order for the dog to mark the fall, and making a sharp noise, such as "Hey," to get the dog's attention before he throws.

Until now, the dog has been accustomed to your throwing; with the change, the lessons must revert to bare ground. In the beginning, it is very likely that the dog will attempt to deliver the dummy to the helper. But, if you instruct him beforehand to remain motionless and double your own whistling, clapping and running antics, this can be overcome immediately.

As soon as you think the dog

Your Labrador puppy should first be introduced to water by letting him walk through a shallow brook. If gradually introduced to deep water, a Lab will eventually be difficult to keep out of it.

has caught on to the change, head back to cover. At the start, shorten the retrieves and work into the wind. When he has progressed to the stage where he is going out 90 yards both on land and water, hunting the area of the fall until he finds the object, and returning with enthusiasm, he is ready to be steadied and taught to deliver to hand.

STEADYING THE LABRADOR

Gradually, you have been increasing the length between the up to five and then send your dog. If he should move beforehand, do your utmost to catch him. If he is too fast and escapes, instruct your helper to pick up the dummy immediately. Then you can bring him back to the starting point, tell him to sit, and reprimand him. But if he gets the dummy and brings it to you, you cannot punish him because he is doing the right thing (but in the wrong way). Always remember that in all forms of dog training, punishment must be administered

This Labrador and his English Springer Spaniel friend are practicing retrieves in the water.

time the dummy hits the ground and when you send your Labrador to retrieve. When he will sit for about five seconds without the slightest struggle and still retain his enthusiasm, he is ready to be steadied. This means sitting without being held until he gets the signal to retrieve.

Tell him firmly to sit, then signal your helper to throw. Count immediately after the misdeed. After a while, you will be able to recognize standard signals your dog gives before he breaks, such as a slight raising of the hindquarters or straightening of the tail. On the first evidence of a signal, repeat a firm "sit" command. The average Labrador grasps this quickly because of his thorough obedience schooling, but sometimes it is necessary to take stronger measures. A check cord attached to his collar works wonders and usually requires use only once. The method is to let the dog go a few yards and then to pull on the rope. A firm footing and a pair of gloves are useful props.

DELIVERING TO HAND

This means that he is to hold the dummy until you take it from him. The command for this is "Fetch!" Have the dog sit; open his mouth and put in the dummy, repeating the command. If he tries to spit it out, hold his mouth closed and say "Fetch!" repeatedly. The first few times, make him hold it for only a few seconds. After the first lesson you

Labs take to the water well and with great enthusiasm. This eager dog has just retrieved a Mallard duck.

When training for water retrieves, an experienced water dog can serve as a good example for your pup to follow.

can gradually decrease the pressure of your hands until just a few taps under the lower jaw will accomplish the purpose. When he associates the action with the command, move away from him, making him "Fetch!" on his own. Then call him to you and take the dummy, following up the action with the usual reward of praise.

DOUBLE RETRIEVES

Lessons must again revert to the lawn. Have your helper go out about 30 yards. He should throw first, and his dummy must fall close to where yours will fall. Send the dog at once. Give him the "Come!" whistle the second he picks up your short dummy; wait to send him for the long fall until his attention is focused in that direction. Sometimes it is necessary to have the helper throw the long dummy again.

When the dog grasps that there are two objects to retrieve, he is often tempted to bring them both in at the same time. Your long-suffering helper should be alerted beforehand of this possibility. The moment he sees the dog heading toward him with the short dummy still in his mouth, he must grab his dummy and conceal it, replacing it only after the dog is on his way back to you.

Occasionally it is necessary to again resort to the check cord to convince the dog that this practice is not the proper method of approach. If this is the case, yank on the check cord before the retrieve and remove it after he has delivered the short dummy.

After three or four lessons on the lawn the average pupil is ready for doubles in cover.

DOUBLES IN WATER

Never attempt water doubles until the dog is completely over the temptation of bringing both dummies at once. At first they should be short retrieves and thrown to fall a wide distance apart.

INTRODUCTION TO THE GUN

There is no excuse for having a gun-shy dog. All that is necessary are a few precautionary measures. The earlier a dog is accustomed to loud noises, the better it is. This conditioning can start in puppyhood by banging on a pan or slamming a door during mealtime. This way loud noises

will be associated with pleasure from the start.

The first time a shotgun is introduced, it should be from a distance and accompanied by something to retrieve. Gradually the distance can be decreased.

INTRODUCTION TO FEATHERS

This should follow the same routine as the dummy introduction. A pigeon is the best bird to begin with, since it is most easily managed by a young dog. It is a good idea to fasten the wings to the body with elastic bands so that the dog will learn to take a good hold from the beginning. After he learns to handle pigeons, other game birds can be used.

LEARNING TO TRAIL

A wing-clipped duck is the best bird to start with, because it has by far the strongest scent. Let the duck have about a minute head start and then lead your dog to the spot where the trail begins. Give him the command to retrieve; in the beginning, if need be, follow along behind him with encouraging words. Be especially careful not to let him get in the habit of backtrailing. Gradually increase the length of the trails by letting the duck have more of a head start. When your Labrador can follow a downwind trail for a distance of 70 yards or more, he is ready for pheasants.

INTRODUCTION TO DECOYS

The easiest way to accustom a dog to decoys is to lay some on the lawn and walk him through them at heel. All investigations

Labs are a joy to work with in the field. They learn quickly and easily.

A properly trained Lab will hold the retrieve in his mouth until given the command to put it in his trainer's hand.

should be discouraged by a firm, repeated "No!"

The next step is to toss a dummy to land beyond the decoys, so that he must go through them to retrieve. If he should grab a decoy instead of a dummy, replace it, repeating "No!," and throw the dummy again. When he ignores the decoys completely on land, repeat the exercise in the water.

RETRIEVING ACROSS WATER AND ROADS, THROUGH FENCES, CHANGES OF COVER

All retrieving done through or across natural hazards must be simply introduced. Begin with a short single. Once the dog understands and can sufficiently cope with the new problem, the distance and number of retrieves can increase.

TEACHING THE DOG TO TAKE A LINE AND TO OBEY HAND SIGNALS

This is essential knowledge for the shooting dog, for it is the only way that he can retrieve birds he has not seen fall. Since the dog has been accustomed to getting a line to a fall from the beginning of his training, he will naturally connect the hand and voice signal with something to retrieve. But the problem is getting him to run a straight line indefinitely when he has not seen anything fall. In the early stages of learning line running, a straight stretch of road or a fence can be employed as a guide. The dummy should be placed beforehand, within plain sight of the starting point. Have the dog sit and line him out. Be sure he sees the dummy before you give him the command to retrieve. Gradually lengthen the distance of these "blind retrieves" until he will go out in a straight line for a distance of a hundred yards. When you think your dog is in the habit of running a straight line, try him in an open field without the former guide. Shorten up on the length at first.

Hand signals are simply a branch of obedience training and can be started as soon as the dog is steady and knows his "Sit-stay," "Heel," "Sit," and "Come" to the whistle. But they must be completely divorced from field work until the dog has fully developed his marking and hunting ability.

Like early lessons in retrieving, the hand signals should begin on bare ground. Sit the dog, then walk about 40 yards away from him. Throw a dummy so that it lands to the right and at an equal distance between you and your Labrador. Then give him the "Come" whistle. When he has progressed about 20 yards toward you, give him the "Sit" whistle. As soon as he sits, throw your right arm out to the side and command, "Over!" By switching arms, the same routine follows for the left direction. The signal for getting directly back is an arm held straight up, accompanied by the command, "Back!"

Labrador Retrievers have an inherent desire to work, and they most enjoy the company of the person who trains them.

The next step, still on bare ground, is to lay the dummies out beforehand in a triangular position. Then place the dog slightly above the base of the triangle and midway between the right and left dummies. Before each signal, give the "Come" whistle, and when he has advanced to the base of the triangle, the "Sit" whistle, followed in a few seconds by a hand signal. Mix up the sequence, first over right, then back, then over left,

Labrador Retrievers can be trained to retrieve on land as well as in water.

and then reversing it. Gradually lengthen the size of the triangle, until the dog is used to going 50 yards or so in one direction.

When he has thoroughly digested the hand signals and is proficient at running a line, the two can be incorporated. The "blind retrieve" should be short to start and set up so that the wind blows across it. Line the dog well to the downwind side of the bird, and when he reaches the spot where the wind will help him,

stop him with the "Sit" whistle and give him the proper "Over" signal. Once he is carrying out all the signals close in with the help of the wind, start increasing the length and including all the directional signals in one retrieve.

TEACHING THE LABRADOR TO QUARTER AND TO FLUSH GAME

Although the Labrador is primarily a retriever, he possesses the intelligence and innate ability to make a top-notch hunter. With a slight amount of prompting, most Labradors will take quite naturally to working like a spaniel. But this phase of their training must be withheld until they have become thoroughly skilled in marking, working out the area of a fall, running a line, and taking directions.

First of all, it is essential to secure the services of a reliable pigeon shot, a couple of pigeons, and a good-size field with medium cover. Make sure the dog is where he cannot see any of the proceedings. Then, dizzy one of the pigeons and plant it in a thick spot of cover out about 150 yards. When you have collected your gun, friend and dog, start out in the direction of the bird; after a few yards, tell the dog to "Hie on!" When he gets about 20 yards out, stop him with the "Sit" whistle and give him the "Over" direction. Keeping him always in gun range as you walk, cast him first to one side and then the other, thus quartering the field, until you have reached the area of the planted pigeon. As he approaches the spot, sneak up and get ready to give the "Sit" whistle the second the bird is flushed. If he should ignore the whistle and chase after the bird, tell your friend to hold shot. Run out immediately and grab the dog, bring him back to the spot, repeat the command and reprimand him. But, if all goes well, let your friend shoot and the dog retrieve.

A good Labrador Retriever must know how to hold a bird without damaging or even ruffling the bird's feathers.

Labrador Retriever judging is underway at the Westminster Kennel Club Dog Show, the most prestigious dog show in the United States.

SHOWING YOUR LABRADOR

A show Labrador Retriever is a comparatively rare thing. He is one out of several litters of puppies. He happens to be born with a degree of physical perfection that closely approximates the standard by which the breed is judged in the show ring. Such a dog should, on maturity, be able to win or approach his championship in good, fast company at the larger shows. Upon finishing his championship, he is apt to be as highly desirable as a breeding animal. As a proven stud, he will automatically command a high price for service.

Showing Labrador Retrievers is a lot of fun—yes, but it is a highly competitive sport. While all the experts were once beginners, the odds are against a novice. You will be showing against experienced

If you plan on showing your Labrador Retriever, you must train him to stand in a proper show pose for judging.

handlers, often people who have devoted a lifetime to breeding, picking the right ones, and then showing those dogs through to their championships. Moreover, the most perfect Labrador Retriever ever born has faults, and in your hands the faults will be far more evident than with the experienced handler who knows how to minimize his Labrador Retriever's faults. These are but a few points on the sad side of the picture.

The experienced handler, as I say, was not born knowing the ropes. He learned—*and so can you!* You can if you will put in the same time, study and keen observation that he did. But it will take time!

KEY TO SUCCESS

First, search for a truly fine show prospect. Take the puppy home, raise him by the book, and as carefully as you know how, give him every chance to mature into the Labrador Retriever you hoped for. My advice is to keep your dog out of big shows, even Puppy Classes, until he is mature. Maturity in the male is roughly two years; with the female, 14 months or so. When your Labrador Retriever is approaching maturity, start out at match shows, and, with this experience for both of you, then go gunning for the big wins at the big shows.

Next step, read the standard by which the Labrador Retriever is judged. Study it until you know it by heart. Having done this, and while your puppy is at home (where he should be) growing into

a normal, healthy Labrador Retriever, go to every dog show you can possibly reach. Sit at the ringside and watch Labrador Retriever judging. Keep your ears and eyes open. Do your own judging, holding each of those dogs against the standard, which you now know by heart.

In your evaluations, don't start looking for faults. Look for the virtues—the best qualities. How does a given Labrador Retriever shape up against the standard? Having looked for and noted the virtues, then note the faults and see what prevents a given Labrador Retriever from standing correctly or moving well. Weigh these faults against the virtues, since, ideally, every feature of the dog should contribute to the harmonious whole dog.

"RINGSIDE JUDGING"

It's a good practice to make notes on each Labrador Retriever, always holding the dog against the standard. In "ringside judging," forget your personal preference for this or that feature. What does the standard say about it? Watch carefully as the judge places the dogs in a given class. It is difficult from the ringside always to see why number one was placed over the second dog. Try to follow the judge's reasoning. Later try to talk with the judge after he is finished. Ask him questions as to why he placed certain Labrador Retrievers and not others. Listen while the judge explains his placings, and, I'll say right here, any judge worthy of his license should be able to give reasons.

This is Ch. Finchingfield Freedom II being exhibited at an outdoor dog show.

When you're not at the ringside, talk with the fanciers. Don't be afraid to ask opinions or say that you don't know. You have a lot of listening to do, and it will help you a great deal and speed up your personal progress if you are a good listener.

THE NATIONAL CLUB

You will find it worthwhile to join the National Labrador Retriever club and to subscribe to its magazine. From the national club, you will learn the location of an approved regional club near you. Now, when your young Labrador Retriever is eight to ten months old, find out the dates of match shows in

enter your Labrador Retriever in as many match shows as you can. When in the ring, you have two jobs. One is to see to it that your Labrador Retriever is always being seen to its best advantage. The other job is to keep your eye on the judge to see what he may want you to do next. Watch only the judge and your Labrador Retriever. Be quick and be alert; do exactly as the judge directs. Don't speak to him except to answer his questions. If he does something you don't like, don't say so. And don't irritate the judge (and everybody else) by constantly talking and fussing with your dog.

Two yellow Labradors patiently await their turn in the show ring.

your section of the country. These differ from regular shows only in that no championship points are given. These shows are especially designed to launch young dogs (and new handlers) on a show career.

ENTER MATCH SHOWS

With the ring deportment you have watched at big shows firmly in mind and practice,

In moving about the ring, remember to keep clear of dogs beside you or in front of you. It is my advice to you *not* to show your Labrador Retriever in a regular point show until he is at least close to maturity and after both you and your dog have had time to perfect ring manners and poise in the match shows.

YOUR LABRADOR'S HEALTH

We know our pets, their moods and habits, and therefore we can recognize when our Labrador Retriever is experiencing an off-day. Signs of sickness can be very obvious or very subtle. As any mother can attest, diagnosing and treating an ailment require common sense, knowing when to seek home remedies and when to visit your doctor ...or veterinarian, as the case may be.

Your veterinarian, we know, is your Labrador Retriever's best friend, next to you. It will pay to be choosy about your veterinarian. Talk to dog owning friends whom you respect. Visit more than one vet before you make a lifelong choice. Trust your instincts. Find a knowledgeable, compassionate vet who knows Labrador Retrievers and likes them.

Grooming for good health makes good sense. The dense Labrador coat benefits from regular brushing to keep looking glossy and clean. Brushing stimulates the natural oils in the coat and also removes dead haircoat. Labradors shed seasonally, which means their undercoat (the soft downy white fur) is pushed out by the incoming new coat. A medium-strength bristle brush and a hound glove are all that is required to groom this natural breed of dog.

A healthy Labrador is a happy Labrador. It is important to maintain your dog's health throughout his entire life.

Anal sacs, sometimes called anal glands, are located in the musculature of the anal ring, one on either side. Each empties into the rectum via a small duct. Occasionally their secretion becomes thickened and accumulates so you can readily feel these structures from the outside. If your Labrador Retriever is scooting across the floor dragging his rear quarters, or licking his rear, his anal sacs may need to be expressed. Placing pressure in and up toward the anus, while holding the tail, is the general routine. Anal sac secretions are characteristically foul-smelling, and you could get squirted if not careful. Veterinarians can take care of this during regular visits and demonstrate the cleanest method.

Labrador Retrievers are predisposed to certain congenital and inherited abnormalities, such as hip dysplasia, a blatantly common problem in purebred dogs with few exceptions. Unfortunately, the Labrador Retriever suffers from a high percentage rate of hip dysplasia despite the efforts of many conscientious breeders. This is due to the breed's unwavering popularity and the careless breeding that surrounds the procreation of such a popular breed. New owners must insist on screening certificates from such hip registries as OFA or PennHIP. Since HD is hereditary, it's necessary to know that the parents and grandparents of your puppy had hips rated good or better. Dysplastic dogs suffer from badly constructed hip joints which become arthritic and very painful, thereby hindering the dog's ability to be a working dog, a good-moving show dog, or even a happy, active pet.

Elbow dysplasia has recently become more of a concern, and the OFA screens for elbows as well. Young dogs typically show signs of limping or rotating elbows when walking or running, which may indicate that elbow dysplasia is present.

Osteochondritis dissecans affects the bones of many large breeds, and although many other breeds are more prone to this disease, the Labrador Retriever has been a victim on many occasions. Panosteitis, affecting bone production, as well as hypertrophic osteodystrophy and myasthenia gravis are also reported as potential bone diseases in the Labrador.

Eye conditions such as cataracts, retinal and vitreal dysplasia, and progressive retinal atrophy have become concerns for Labrador breeders. Screening for eye problems has therefore been prioritized. PRA, the most frequently encountered eye disease in Labradors, is an inherited defect that can severely reduce a dog's vision. Retinal dysplasia ultimately ends in blindness and is an inherited disease. Entropion and ectropion, both affecting the eyelids, affect Labradors, as does distichiasis (extra eyelashes). All of these can be corrected through surgerythough eliminate the dog from competing in dog shows.

Von Willebrand's disease, a bleeding disorder, and hemophilia A are conditions that affect many dog breeds and do not exclude the Labrador Retriever.

Epilepsy, a possible hereditary condition that is linked to the brain's receiving incorrect stimulus, hinders many breeds of dog and is problematic in Labradors. Affected dogs show signs of mild seizures between six months and three years. Although incurable, fits can be treated with medication.

Despite the preceding list of possible genetic diseases, the Labrador is a healthy, long-lived companion animal. Proper care and education can only help owners promote the health and longevity of their dogs. Most breeders advise against feeding the Labrador Retriever one large meal per day because of the dangers of bloat (gastric torsion): the twisting of the stomach causes gas to build up and the organ expands like a balloon. Avoiding strenuous exercise and large amounts of water can preclude the occurrence of bloat, as can feeding two smaller meals instead of one larger one. A good commercial dog food is recommended for the dog's balanced diet.

For the continued health of your dog, owners must attend to vaccinations regularly. Your veterinarian can recommend a vaccination schedule appropriate for your dog, taking into consideration the factors of climate and geography. The basic vaccinations to protect your dog are: parvovirus, distemper,

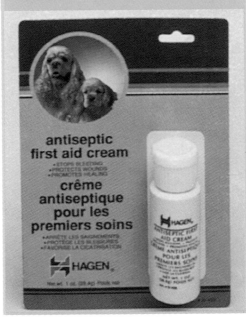

Keep this first aid cream on hand in cases of cuts as it is antiseptic. Photo courtesy of Hagen.

hepatitis, leptospirosis, adenovirus, parainfluenza, coronavirus, bordetella, tracheobronchitis (kennel cough), Lyme disease and rabies.

Parvovirus is a highly contagious, dog-specific disease, first recognized in 1978. Targeting the small intestine, parvo affects the stomach, and diarrhea and vomiting (with blood) are clinical signs. Although the dog can pass the infection to other dogs within three days of infection, the initial signs, which include lethargy and depression, don't display themselves until four to seven days. When affecting puppies under four weeks of age, the heart muscle is frequently attacked. When the heart is affected, the puppies exhibit difficulty in breathing and experience crying and foaming at the nose and mouth.

Distemper, related to human measles, is an airborne virus that spreads in the blood and ultimately in the nervous system and epithelial tissues. Young dogs or dogs with weak immune systems can develop encephalomyelitis (brain disease) from the distemper infection. Such dogs experience seizures, general weakness and rigidity, as well as "hardpad." Since distemper is largely incurable, prevention through vaccination is vitally important. Puppies should be vaccinated at six to eight weeks of age, with boosters at ten to 12 weeks. Older puppies (16 weeks and older) who are unvaccinated should receive no fewer than two vaccinations at three- to four-week intervals.

Hepatitis mainly affects the liver and is caused by canine adenovirus type I. Highly infectious, hepatitis often affects dogs nine to 12 months of age. Initially the virus localizes in the dog's tonsils and then disperses to the liver, kidney and eyes. Generally speaking the dog's immune system is capable of combating this virus. Canine infectious hepatitis affects dogs whose systems cannot fight off the adenovirus. Affected dogs have fever, abdominal pains, bruising on mucous membranes and gums, and experience comas and convulsions. Prevention of hepatitis exists only through vaccination at eight to ten weeks of age and then boosters three or four weeks later, then annually.

Leptospirosis is a bacterium-related disease, often spread by rodents. The organisms that spread leptospirosis enter through the mucous membranes and spread to the internal organs via the bloodstream. It can be passed through the dog's urine. Leptospirosis does not affect

young dogs as consistently as do the other viruses; it is reportedly regional in distribution and somewhat dependent on the immunostatus of the dog. Fever, inappetence, vomiting, dehydration, hemorrhage, kidney and eye disease can result in moderate cases.

Bordetella, called canine cough, causes a persistent hacking cough in dogs and is very contagious. Bordetella involves a virus and a bacteria: parainfluenza is the most common virus implicated; *Bordetella bronchiseptica*, the bacterium. Bronchitis and pneumonia result in less than 20 percent of the cases, and most dogs recover from the condition within a week to four weeks. Non-prescription medicines can help relieve the hacking cough, though nothing can cure the condition before it's run its course. Vaccination cannot guarantee protection from canine cough, but it does ward off the most common virus responsible for the condition.

Lyme disease (also called borreliosis), although known for decades, was only first diagnosed in dogs in 1984. Lyme disease can affect cats, cattle, and horses, but especially people. In the US, the disease is transmitted by two ticks carrying the *Borrelia burgdorferi* organism: the deer tick (*Ixodes scapularis*) and the western black-legged tick (*Ixodes pacificus*), the latter primarily affects reptiles. In Europe, *Ixodes ricinus* is responsible for spreading Lyme. The disease causes lameness, fever, joint swelling, inappetence, and lethargy. Removal of ticks from the dog's coat can help reduce the chances of Lyme, though not as much as avoiding heavily wooded areas where the dog is most likely to contract ticks. A vaccination is available, though it has not been proven to protect dogs from all strains of the organism that causes the disease.

Rabies is passed to dogs and people through wildlife: in North America, principally through the skunk, fox and raccoon; the bat is not the culprit it was once thought to be. Likewise, the common image of the rabid dog foaming at the mouth with every hair on end is unlikely the truest scenario. A rabid dog exhibits difficulty eating, salivates much and has spells of paralysis and awkwardness. Before a dog reaches this final state, it may experience anxiety, personality changes, irritability and more aggressiveness than is usual. Vaccinations are strongly recommended as rabid dogs are too dangerous to manage and are commonly euthanized. Puppies are generally vaccinated at 12 weeks of age, and then annually. Although rabies is on the decline in the world community, tens of thousands of humans die each year from rabies-related incidents.

Parasites have clung to our pets for centuries. Despite our modern efforts, fleas still pester our pet's existence, and our own. All dogs itch, and fleas can make even the happiest dog a miserable, scabby mess. The loss of hair and habitual biting and chewing at themselves rank among the annoyances; the nuisances include the passing of tapeworms and the whole family's itching through the summer months. A full range of flea-control and elimination products are available at pet shops, and your veterinarian surely has recommendations. Sprays, powders, collars and dips fight fleas from the outside; drops and pills fight the good fight from inside. Discuss the possibilities with your vet. Not all products can be used in conjunction with one another, and some dogs may be more sensitive to certain applications than others. The dog's living quarters must be debugged as well as the dog itself. Heavy infestation may require multiple treatments.

Always check your dog for ticks carefully. Although fleas can be acquired almost anywhere, ticks are more likely to be picked up in heavily treed areas, pastures or other outside grounds (such as dog shows or obedience or field trials). Athletic, active, and hunting dogs are the most likely subjects, though any passing dog can be the host. Remember Lyme disease is passed by tick infestation.

As for internal parasites, worms are potentially dangerous for dogs and people. Roundworms, hookworms, whipworms, tapeworms, and heartworms comprise the blightsome party of troublemakers. Deworming puppies begins at around two to three weeks and continues until three months of age. Proper hygienic care of the environment is also important to prevent contamination with roundworm and hookworm eggs. Heartworm preventatives are recommended by most veterinarians, although there are some drawbacks to the regular introduction of poisons into our dogs' system. These daily or monthly preparations also help regulate most other worms as well. Discuss worming procedures with your veterinarian.

Roundworms pose a great threat to dogs and people. They are found in the intestine of dogs and can be passed to people

A full range of flea-control products is available at pet shops, and your veterinarian surely has recommendations as well. Photo courtesy of Hagen.

through ingestion of feces-contaminated dirt. Roundworm infection can be prevented by not walking dogs in heavy-traffic people areas, by burning feces, and by curbing dogs in a responsible manner. (Of course, in most areas of the country, curbing dogs is the law.) Roundworms are typically passed from the bitch to the litter, and bitches should be treated along with the puppies, even if she tested negative prior to whelping. Generally puppies are treated every two weeks until two months of age.

Hookworms, like roundworms, are also a danger to dogs and people. The hookworm parasite (known as *Ancylostoma caninum*) causes cutaneous larva migrans in people. The eggs of hookworms are passed in feces and become infective in shady, sandy areas. The larvae penetrate the skin of the dog, and the dog subsequently becomes infected. When swallowed, these parasites affect the intestines, lungs, windpipe, and the whole digestive system. Infected dogs suffer from anemia and lose large amounts of blood in the places where the worms latch onto the dog's intestines, etc.

Although infrequently passed to humans, whipworms are cited as one of the most common parasites in America. These elongated worms affect the intestines of the dog, where they latch on, and cause colic upset or diarrhea. Unless identified in stools passed, whipworms are difficult to diagnose. Adult worms can be eliminated more consistently than the larvae, since whipworms exhibit unusual life cycles. Proper hygienic care of outdoor grounds is critical to the avoidance of these harmful parasites.

Tapeworms are carried by fleas, and enter the dog when the dog swallows the flea. Humans can acquire tapeworms in the same way, though we are less likely to swallow fleas than dogs are. Recent studies have shown that certain rodents and other wild animals have been infected with tapeworms, and dogs can be affected by catching and/or eating these other animals. Of course, outdoor hunting dogs and terriers are more likely to be infected in this way than are your typical house dog or non-motivated hound. Treatment for tapeworm has proven very effective, and infected dogs do not show great discomfort or symptoms. When people are infected, however, the liver can be seriously damaged. Proper cleanliness is the best bet against tapeworms.

Heartworm disease is transmitted by mosquitoes and badly affects the lungs, heart and blood vessels of dogs. The larvae of *Dirofilaria immitis* enters the dog's bloodstream when bitten by an infected mosquito. The larvae takes about six months to mature. Infected dogs suffer from weight loss, appetite loss, chronic coughing and general fatigue. Not all affected dogs show signs of illness right away, and carrier dogs may be affected for years before clinical signs appear. Treatment of heartworm disease has been effective but can be dangerous also. Prevention as always is the desirable alternative. Ivermectin is the active ingredient in most heartworm preventatives and

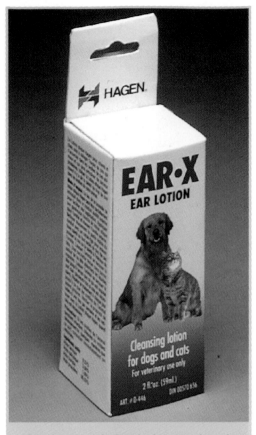

Keeping your Labrador's ears clean is simple if you use a top-quality lotion. It is essential that you maintain your dogs' ears, claws, mouth and fur. Photo courtesy of Hagen.

has proven to be successful. Check with your veterinarian for the preparation that is best for your dog. Dogs generally begin taking the preventatives at eight months of age and continue to do so throughout the non-winter months.

The Publisher wishes to acknowledge the cooperation of the following owners whose dogs are portrayed in this book: Dianne Ammerman, Biddle Knls, Lori A. Brittle, Connaughton Knls, Gordon Knls, Fred Grazioso, Nancy Horvath, Bonnie Kellner, Pamela C. Kelsey, George and Lillian Knobloch, Kathy and Ted McCue, Myers Knls, Holly and Judie Niece, Sonya Ninneman, Frank Purdy, Dianne L. Schlemmer, David W. Schnare, Deb Tirmenlon, and Stephen Wojculewski (agent).

OTHER BOOKS ON THE LABRADOR RETRIEVER BY TFH PUBLICATIONS, INC.

TS-241

TW-140

H-1059

PS-805

Labrador Retriever owners will find complete coverage of the breed in four special books by T.F.H. Publications. The newest of these are *The Official Book of the Labrador Retriever* by the Labrador Retriever Club, Inc. and *The Proper Care of Labrador Retrievers* by Dennis and Pat Livesey. *The Book of the Labrador Retriever* and *The Labrador Retriever* are also valuable reading on the breed and remain necessary volumes in any Labrador lover's library.

INDEX